Micro Knowledge

written by JOHN SMITH B Sc(ENG), M Ed
*Department of Creative Design,
Loughborough University of Technology*

illustrations by KEN McKIE

Ladybird Books Loughborough

Counting in Binary

A good starting point is to see how your micro counts. A computer can only tell if something inside it is on or off. Think of it like a light bulb. If it's ON we can call that ONE. If it's OFF we can call that ZERO.

Suppose we have two light bulbs. How many different patterns of ON and OFF can we have?

Making number 1 stand for ON and number 0 stand for OFF we can turn this into a system for counting.

both OFF
right ON
left ON
both ON

twos	units	
0	0	we say is 0
0	1	represents 1
1	0	represents 2
1	1	represents 3

So we can only count up to three with two bulbs. With three light bulbs we can count to seven. We call this BINARY counting. Just like a **bi**cycle has TWO wheels and **bi**noculars have TWO lenses, **bi**nary counting uses only TWO numbers. So you can only count with 0 and 1.

People are used to counting using TEN numbers: 0,1,2,3,4,5,6,7,8,9. The word for counting with TEN numbers is DECimal from the Latin *decem* meaning ten.

In binary counting, each digit is known as a BIT (short for **BI**NARY DIG**IT**). The binary number 101 is a three BIT number.

Let's try converting some binary numbers to decimal numbers

Suppose we have a binary number with four bits, say 1010.

We can set it out like this:

eights	fours	twos	units
1	0	1	0

Notice that each column heading is two times more than the one to its right. To convert 1010 to decimal we just read off the columns where there's a 1 and add the decimal values together. Like this:

eights	fours	twos	units	
1	0	1	0	
8 +	0 +	2 +	0	= 10 (ten)

Using these columns, what's the largest four bit number we can make?

Yes, it's 1111:

eights	fours	twos	units	
1	1	1	1	
			=	?

What is this in decimal? Add up the columns and see!

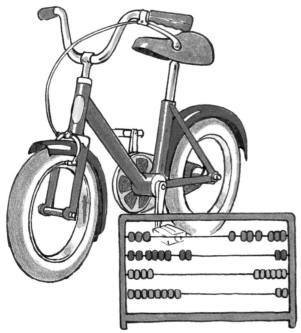

The table below shows all the possible binary numbers using four bits, ie the equivalent of 0 to 15.

Binary	Decimal
0000	0
0001	1
0010	2
0011	3
0100	4
0101	5
0110	6
0111	7
1000	8
1001	9
1010	10
1011	11
1100	12
1101	13
1110	14
1111	15

We can of course start with a decimal number and convert it to binary.

Here's a program to help you. This program will change decimal numbers (up to 15) to the equivalent four bit binary numbers.

```
10 MODE 6
15  REM Print information heading starting 4 lines down.
20 PRINT TAB(0,4)"This program will change a decimal"
30 PRINT "number between 0 and 15 to its "
40 PRINT "binary equivalent."
45  REM Leave a line.
50 PRINT
60 PRINT "Type in a decimal number between"
65  REM Number to be decoded is input and stored in N.
70 INPUT "0 and 15 and press RETURN   "N
75  REM Decoding of decimal number.
80 IF N<0 OR N>15 THEN 10
90 IF N>7 THEN D=1 ELSE D=0
100 IF D=1 THEN M=N-8 ELSE M=N
110 IF M>3 THEN C=1 ELSE C=0
120 IF C=1 THEN P=M-4 ELSE P=M
130 IF P>1 THEN B=1 ELSE B=0
140 IF B=1 THEN Q=P-2 ELSE Q=P
150 IF Q>0 THEN A=1 ELSE A=0
155  REM Print headings.
160 PRINT TAB(10,15)"DECIMAL"
170 PRINT TAB(21,15)"BINARY"
175  REM Print decimal number.
180 PRINT TAB(13,17);N
185  REM Print BITs of binary equivalent.
190 PRINT TAB(22,17);D;C;B;A
200 PRINT TAB(0,20)"Do you wish to check another number?"
210 PRINT "(Y/N)"
215  REM Next letter or number pressed is stored in yn$ if pressed within 40 seconds.
220 yn$ = INKEY$(4000)
225  REM If you press y or Y you can try a new number.  If not program will end having printed goodbye.
230 IF  yn$="Y" OR yn$ ="y" THEN 10 ELSE CLS
240 PRINT TAB(5,5)"GOODBYE"
250 END
```

What's the biggest number your computer can store and handle? Most home computers today are 8 bit; they count as though they have sets of eight light bulbs to turn ON and OFF inside. Using sets of eight bits, computers can handle whole numbers as large as two thousand million (2,000,000,000).

Of course, the computer doesn't use light bulbs. Remember, the parts that go on and off are called BITS. You may have heard people talk about 8 bit, 16 bit and even 32 bit micro computers. The micro computer that you use at present is probably an 8 bit machine. Eight bits are often known as a BYTE.

Later in the book we shall want to know the decimal equivalent of a BYTE so let's try a few examples here.

Consider the number 11111111.

128	64	32	16	8	4	2	1	
1	1	1	1	1	1	1	1	
128 + 64 + 32 + 16 + 8 + 4 + 2 + 1 = 255								

Now try another.

128	64	32	16	8	4	2	1	
1	0	0	0	0	0	0	1	
128 + 0 + 0 + 0 + 0 + 0 + 0 + 1 = 129								

Now you work out 10001000.

Yes! The answer is 136.

Working out 8 bit numbers is quite difficult so computer people sometimes use a special code called HEXADECIMAL.

Counting in hexadecimal

Have you noticed that when a large program is loading from a cassette into the BBC micro some 'funny' numbers appear on the screen?

It starts like this...01,02,03,...09

What happens after 09? The next figure is not 10 as you might expect, but it is 0A!

The counting continues...
0A,0B,0C,0D,0E,0F,10,11,12,13...
1E,1F...and so on.

What is happening?

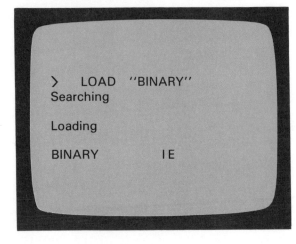

```
>   LOAD  "BINARY"
Searching

Loading

BINARY           1E
```

When we count we use ten single digits (decimal):—

0	1	2	3	4	5	6	7	8	9

Each number is one digit, six is 6 and three is 3.

What happens when we reach ten?

0	1	2	3	4	5	6	7	8	9	**10**

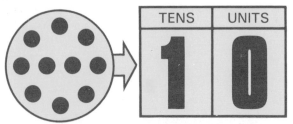

When we get to ten we haven't got any more single digits. We convert our ten units to a single TEN and no UNITS and use two digits.

We can think of the computer counting in sets of four bits. We saw that with four bits we can count from 0 to 15 (16 numbers.)

The code used to count in groups of sixteen numbers is called HEXADECIMAL. (Remember, a HEXagon has SIX sides, so hexadecimal is 6 + 10 or 16.)

0 1 2 3 4 5 6 7 8 9...

WHAT'S NEXT?

(No one has yet invented single digit numerals beyond 9.)

What computer people have done is to use letters to represent the rest of the counting in hexadecimal. So, counting in hex (short for hexadecimal) looks like this...

0 1 2 3 4 5 6 7 8 9 A B C D E F

In the hex code, F stands for 15 and A for 10. What does C stand for?

We can now look at three ways of counting.

Binary	Hexadecimal	Decimal
0000	0	0
0001	1	1
0010	2	2
0011	3	3
0100	4	4
0101	5	5
0110	6	6
0111	7	7
1000	8	8
1001	9	9
1010	A	10
1011	B	11
1100	C	12
1101	D	13
1110	E	14
1111	F	15
10000	10	16

10001 – *What would this number be in hexadecimal and decimal?*

REMEMBER!

BINARY is used by the computer in all its workings.

HEXADECIMAL is the name of the code used for counting using sixteen digits.

DECIMAL is the way we are used to counting in everyday life and it uses ten single digits.

Don't forget that ZERO is a number too!

So when we see a BBC computer loading a program from cassette we are watching it count in hexadecimal or groups of sixteen.

Why not load your favourite program and watch the screen as it loads the program into memory? Count as it loads and you'll be counting in hexadecimal.

This explains the mystery of the 'funny' numbers!

Most computers accept numbers in decimal or in hexadecimal and then convert them into binary. It's easier for people to work in decimal rather than hexadecimal, so let's see the computer change numbers from hex to decimal and back again.

Type in:

MODE2 and press RETURN
PRINT &F and press RETURN*

You should get 15.

(We are working in MODE 2 because in MODE 7 the symbol $\sim$, used later, will appear as ÷. Putting & in front of the number tells the computer you are typing a hexadecimal code.)

*After typing in any instructions the RETURN key should of course be pressed. This symbol will remind you.

Try another one,

```
MODE2                    RETURN
PRINT &FF                RETURN
```

Did the number 255 appear on the screen?

So you can see it is very easy to translate from hexadecimal to decimal, using your computer.

If you want to go the other way (to find the hexadecimal equivalent of a decimal number) then you use ∼ .

Type in: `PRINT ∼ 15`   RETURN

The answer should be F.

(∼ means find the hexadecimal code for this number. If you see ÷ on the screen, it means you are still in MODE 7.)

Try: `PRINT ∼ 10`   RETURN

and: `PRINT ∼ 17`   RETURN

This will give you the hex equivalent of decimal 10 and decimal 17.

Now we can count in binary like a computer. We are able to change a binary number into a hexadecimal number and then back again.

Here's a game you can try to test your skill with these new sorts of numbers. The computer prints out a binary number on the screen. You have to work out what it is in decimal and type in your answer.

```
10 DIM X(5)
20 MODE 4
30 decimal = RND(15)
40 CLS
50 PRINT TAB(0,4)"Type in ALL four bits of the ":PRINT
60 PRINT "BINARY number which is equivalent":PRINT
70 PRINT "to the given DECIMAL number."
80 PRINT TAB(8,12)"DECIMAL"; TAB(27,12)"BINARY"
90 PRINT TAB(28,14)"****"
100 PRINT TAB(11,14);decimal
110  VDU 31,28,14
120   FOR B = 1 TO 4
130 get=GET
140 IF get =48 THEN X(B) =0
150 IF get =49 THEN X(B) =1
160 IF get <48 OR get>49 THEN 130
170 PRINT TAB(27+B,14);X(B)
180 VDU 31,28+B,14
190   NEXT B
200  VDU 31,5,20
210 binary = X(1)*2^3 +X(2)*2^2 +X(3)*2^1 +X(4)*2^0
220 IF binary =decimal THEN 230 ELSE SOUND 1,-15,33,20
:GOTO 40
230 PRINT TAB(10,20)"WELL":SOUND 1,-15,109,10:SOUND
1,-15,121,40:PRINT TAB(15,20)" DONE"
240 PRINT : PRINT
250 PRINT " DO YOU WANT ANOTHER GO?  (Y/N)"
260 VDU 31,32,23
270 G$ =GET$
280 IF G$ = "Y" OR G$ = "y" THEN 30 ELSE CLS :PRINT
TAB(10,26)"GOODBYE FOR NOW"
290 END
```

Don't press RETURN yet!

ASCII code

How does the computer, only being able to work in 0s and 1s, represent letters of the alphabet and other symbols on your keyboard?

There is a code which allows it to do this and it is very important for computers.

If computers are ever going to talk to each other they need to use the same code. The usual code is called an ASCII code. ASCII, pronounced 'askey', stands for American Standard Code for Information Interchange.

	dec	hex		dec	hex		dec	hex		dec	hex
A	65	41	N	78	4E	a	97	61	n	110	6E
B	66	42	O	79	4F	b	98	62	o	111	6F
C	67	43	P	80	50	c	99	63	p	112	70
D	68	44	Q	81	51	d	100	64	q	113	71
E	69	45	R	82	52	e	101	65	r	114	72
F	70	46	S	83	53	f	102	66	s	115	73
G	71	47	T	84	54	g	103	67	t	116	74
H	72	48	U	85	55	h	104	68	u	117	75
I	73	49	V	86	56	i	105	69	v	118	76
J	74	4A	W	87	57	j	106	6A	w	119	77
K	75	4B	X	88	58	k	107	6B	x	120	78
L	76	4C	Y	89	59	l	108	6C	y	121	79
M	77	4D	Z	90	5A	m	109	6D	z	122	7A

Here's how...

If you type

`PRINT ASC("A")` **RETURN**

it will give you the code for the letter A in decimal.

The computer remembers this as the binary number equal to 65 decimal and hex 41.

That is...

0100 0001

(There is a small space between the two sets of four bits to make it easier to read.)

If you read this binary number as two four bit numbers you will see how we get hex 41. (Look back at page 7.)

0100 0001
  4   1

So the hexadecimal value of 0100 0001 is 41.

Let's try another one.

Type:

`PRINT ASC("G")` **RETURN**

The computer will respond with 71.

G is decimal 71, hex 47 and binary 0100 0111.

That is...   Binary   0100 0111
                      4   7
                    &47

To work out a letter from the binary code you can do this...
                Binary   0100 1011
                       4   B
                   &4B

So 0100 1011 is the same as hex 4B.

Using the computer we can then type:

`PRINT CHR$(&4B)` **RETURN**

The result will be K.

We can check this by looking up hex4B in the ASCII Code table. (See page 10.)

CAN YOU DO THIS?

Below is a secret message written in BINARY ASCII code. See if you can complete the message using the method you've just seen. If you have any problem use a computer to help.

1 Translate the eight bit binary into hexadecimal.

2 Use the computer or the table on page 10 to work out the letter.

eg	0100 0111	0101 0010	0100 0101	0100 0001	0101 0100
	&47	&52	&?	?	?
	G	R	?	?	?

IF YOU'RE STUCK TRY THIS

PRINT CHR$(&▲) [RETURN]
(insert the hexadecimal value)

Type in:

eg PRINT CHR$(&47)   [RETURN]
   this gives 'G'

PRINT CHR$(&52)   [RETURN]
   this gives 'R'

Why not send a message to a friend who is interested in computers?

Try these:

Who invented the first mechanical calculating machine?

0101 0000   0100 0001   0101 0011
0100 0011   0100 0001   0100 1100

Who invented the forerunner of the computer?

0100 0010   0100 0001   0100 0010
0100 0010   0100 0001   0100 0111
0100 0101

Occasionally the ASCII code can be useful when writing programs.

Consider the following which prints out the capital letters of the alphabet.

```
10 MODE 1
20 PRINT "This program will print out the"
25 PRINT
30 PRINT "capital letters of the alphabet."
40  FOR ascii = 65 TO 90
50 PRINT TAB(ascii-62,15)CHR$(ascii)
60 FOR T= 1 TO 500 : NEXT T
70  NEXT ascii
80 PRINT TAB(0,25)"Now, why not make the computer print"
90 PRINT TAB(0,27)"all the small letters e.g. abc?"
100 END
```

Lines 40-70: The ASCII values for capital letters go from 65 to 90.

The FOR NEXT loop makes the number in ascii go from 65 to 90 in steps of 1.

Each time through the loop line 50 prints the letter with the ASCII value currently in ascii. It prints the letter at the position on the screen of (ascii minus 62, 15).

Line 60: is a simple time delay.

Another use is to produce random letters.

```
10 MODE 1
20 random = RND(26)
30 ascii = random + 64
40 PROCdelay(20)
50 PRINT TAB(3,15)"Your random letter this time is:-"
60 PROCdelay(50)
70 PRINT TAB(18,18)CHR$(ascii)
80 PROCdelay(30)
90 PRINT TAB(3,28)"Do you want another letter? (Y/N) "
100 YN$ = GET$
110 IF YN$ = "Y" OR YN$ = "y" THEN 10 ELSE CLS
120 PRINT TAB(10,15)"GOODBYE"
130  END
140 DEF PROCdelay(T)
150  time = TIME
160  REPEAT
170  UNTIL TIME >= time + T
180 ENDPROC
```

Line 20: There are 26 letters in the alphabet and RND(26) selects at random a number between 1 and 26. It is stored in 'random.'

Line 30: The ASCII values for capital letters are between 65(A) and 90(Z) so we add 64 to 'random.'

Line 100: The first letter pressed is stored in YN$.

Lines 140-180: This procedure produces a time delay of the value T $\div$ 100 secs. T is equal to the value in brackets following PROCdelay.

(In line 60 it is 50 so delay is half a second.

In line 80 it is 30 so delay is three tenths of a second)

Memory

A chip

In order for a computer to work, it must have memory. It is no use giving the computer two numbers to add together if it forgets the first number before you give it the second.

Shown below is a photograph of the inside of the BBC microcomputer. There are two main areas of memory which are each made up of a number of integrated circuits (ICs) often known as chips.

The ICs are known as chips because inside the black plastic case is a little chip of silicon containing the memory circuits.

We are going to look at three types of memory: ROM, RAM and EPROM.

RAM

ROMS or EPROMS can be inserted here

ROM

Microprocessor

ROM

ROM stands for 'Read Only Memory'.

As the name suggests the computer can only read this type of memory, it cannot change it.

One advantage of ROM is that it never forgets, even when the electrical supply is removed. Computer people call it *non-volatile memory* – it never disappears. The instructions which tell the computer how to run a program are stored in a ROM.

The computer has to know the location of these instructions and other information.

You can think of a location as one of a set of pigeon holes in a letter rack. Letters for Mrs James would be put in the hole labelled 'J' and Mr Brown's would, of course, be in the hole 'B'. The labels 'J' and 'B' are the addresses.

In this special letter rack, only one envelope can be stored in a location (pigeon hole) at any one time.

If you like, you can have a look at what is stored in one of the locations in a ROM.

Type in:

```
PRINT ?(65000)
```
RETURN

A number will appear on the screen, probably 255. If you are using the Electron machine the number will probably be 110. This is what is stored in location 65000 in the computer. The number 65000 is one of the ROM addresses.

All locations between 65280 and 65535 are in ROM, so you can look at any of them using the same command.

In PRINT ?(65000) the question mark tells the computer to read what is in a particular location and PRINT tells it to print a copy of the contents on the screen.

The address for the memory is a binary code which for many machines is 16 bits long.

For example 1111 1111 1111 1111.

This means, in hexadecimal, the largest address is &FFFF. In decimal this is 65535.

To find what is stored at this highest address type in

PRINT ?65535   RETURN

Is it 221 (Electron 218)? It might be different for your machine. You will get the same answer if you use

PRINT ?&FFFF   RETURN

Let's see if we can change what is stored in location 65535.

Type in:

?65535 = 100   RETURN

The command ?65535 = 100 says,'Find the location with address 65535 and change its contents to 100.' So if we now look at location 65535 it should contain 100 if the change has been made.

Type in:

PRINT ?65535   RETURN

You should see that the stored value has *not* changed. It is still the same ie in this case, 221 (Electron 218.) The 100 has not been accepted. This is because 65535 is in the Read Only Memory. It can be *read* but not changed.

RAM

There is another type of memory called RAM (Random Access Memory.) This memory *can* be changed. It is easier to understand if you call it *read write memory*. This is because you can put information into it (known as writing to the memory) and then read it back again.

RAM is very useful because we can use this part of the memory over and over again.

LET'S TRY IT

16

We can look to see if there is anything stored in RAM at an address, say 8000.

Type in: `PRINT ?8000`   RETURN

It will be zero unless you have run a program.

Having read this location and found the number zero, let's replace it with your age.

Suppose you are 12 years old.

Type in: `?8000 = 12`   RETURN

This puts 12 in location 8000. Let's see if it's there.

Type in: `PRINT ?8000`   RETURN

Did the computer print your age?

If you try to put in a number greater than 255 it will not work correctly because 255 is the maximum number you can store in an 8 bit memory location. Remember 1111 1111 would be all bits ON and this is 255 decimal.

Try using the age of somebody older than you and put that in location 8000. You can keep doing this. The value stored in a RAM location can be changed over and over again.

The disadvantage of RAM is that if we switch off the computer we lose all the information stored in this type of memory. Computer people say, therefore, that RAM is *volatile memory* – the contents can vanish. That's why you need to save your programs on cassette or disc from RAM so that they won't be lost when the electrical supply is turned off. When you want to use a program again you load it from the tape or disc into the RAM part of the computer's memory.

Switch off your microcomputer and then turn it on again. Look at what is now in the memory at address 65000 in ROM and address 8000 in RAM.

Type in:

PRINT ?65000   RETURN

Is this still the previous value, 255, in the ROM section?

PRINT ?8000   RETURN

Is this 0 in the location 8000 in RAM?

How can we find out which locations are in RAM and which in ROM?

We can use a map!

It's in the *User Guide* if you know how to use it.

A computer memory map is unusual. You can think of it as all the memory locations stacked one above the other like an enormous stack of single pigeon holes.

To find our way about the memory we use this special map.

We have seen that in the BBC machine there are 65535 (&FFFF) locations. These can't all be drawn individually on a page so in the map we just give the addresses which interest us like the top, the bottom and those that divide sections of memory.

You can now see the ROM area, the RAM area and the position of those locations we have already looked at such as 8000 and 65000.

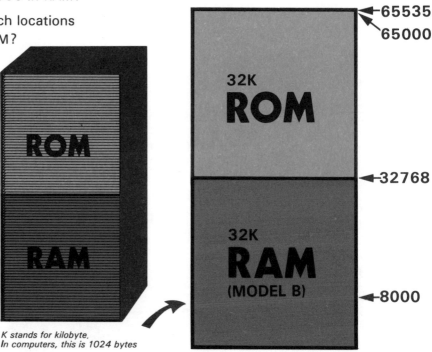

K stands for kilobyte.
In computers, this is 1024 bytes

EPROM

There is another type of memory known as EPROM. It is 'Erasable Programmable Read Only Memory'. In many ways it's like the ROM we have described earlier in that we can store information, such as a program, in it and plug it into the computer. Even if the computer is switched off the contents of the EPROM will remain the same.

If the program which is stored is faulty, it can be rubbed out or *erased* using ultra violet light. The EPROM can then be reprogrammed with the correct information.

ROMS are cheaper than EPROMS when they are made in large quantities, but if there is a mistake in the ROM then it cannot be corrected and usually has to be thrown away.

EPROM

EPROMS can be inserted here

BUSES

Let's look at how the computer finds the memory location which it wants to read or, if it is in RAM, to read or write to.

In practice the microprocessor, the 'heart' of a microcomputer, is connected to all the memory by three sets of wires. Each set of wires is known as a BUS.

The microprocessor uses the ADDRESS bus to identify which memory location it wishes to read or write to.

The DATA bus is used to transmit the data between the memory location and the microprocessor.

The CONTROL bus is used by the microprocessor to ensure that the data is read or written to a location at the correct time.

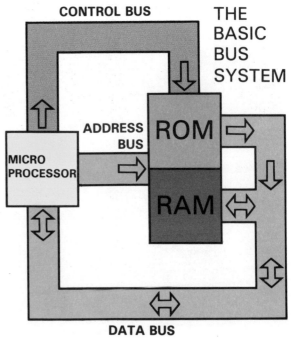

THE BASIC BUS SYSTEM

Let's see how the microprocessor uses the sets of wires to read a memory location.

In the drawing below, the microprocessor has set the number 1000 (decimal 8) on the ADDRESS bus because it wants to read what is in location 8.

When the CONTROL bus is set to read, the DATA bus takes on the value in location 8, ie 0110 (6) which is read by the microprocessor.

What value will appear on the data bus when the address bus is set to 9?

Yes, 1010 (10).

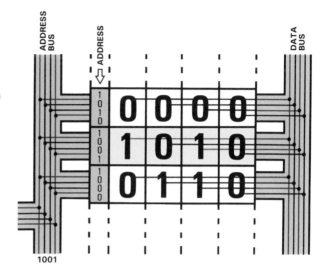

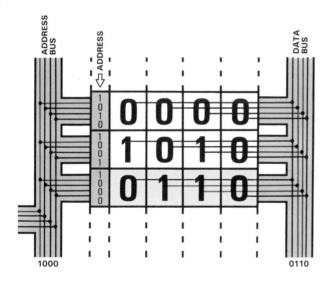

In practice the microprocessor puts a pattern of electrical voltages on the wires of the ADDRESS bus. The patterns of voltages are the same as the 0s and 1s of the address of the location it is looking for. 0 is a low voltage and 1 is a high voltage.

When the appropriate voltage signal is sent on the CONTROL bus, the voltage pattern matching the 0s and 1s of the binary number stored in the location appears on the wires of the DATA bus.

It then uses a single wire to say 'read this location.' An electronic switch connects the memory location to the second BUS, the DATA bus.

A voltage pattern matching the 0s and 1s of the binary number stored in the location appears on the wires of the data bus. This pattern of voltages is recognised by the microprocessor and it now knows the contents of that location. It has 'read' the value.

In this example, we only used a few memory locations and buses with only four wires.

In a real 8 bit computer like the BBC micro, the ADDRESS bus (which has the address of the memory location required) is made up of 16 wires. The second bus, (the DATA bus which can be used to carry information to or from the microprocessor) has 8 wires.

The actual voltages used on the buses are about nought volts for 0 and four volts for 1.

Making Characters

In this section of the book we are going to look at how letters and shapes, ie *characters*, are formed on the screen. The smallest character we usually form is a full stop like this one (.) It uses four dots.

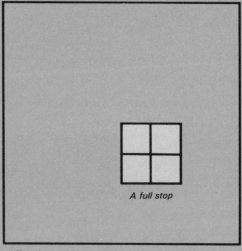

A full stop

Each letter, eg A, H, or X, is formed in a square on the screen known as a *character block*. A character is made up of 8 rows of 8 small squares, each the size of the full stop dots. Each small square, called a pixel, can be ON or OFF.

In the diagram opposite there is a pattern formed in the 8 by 8 squares. Can you see that by choosing which little squares are lit up, we can make a shape?

22

We will now look at how this light green shape opposite is put into the computer.

The shapes for letters and numbers which are on the keyboard are stored in the computer's permanent memory, in ROM, but there are some spaces in RAM where you can store shapes. They are stored under the ASCII code numbers 224 to 255.

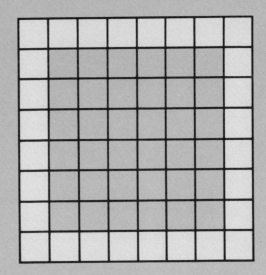

We can make a shape, give it an ASCII number, store it and then print it on the screen when and where we want to.

If we want to store the square shape in ASCII number 251, we use:

```
VDU 23,251,255,129,129,129,129,129,129,255
```

DON'T TYPE THIS IN YET. READ ON!

The following helps to explain all the numbers. The command is in the form:

VDU 23, PART 1	ASCII Number, PART 2	a,b,c,d,e,f,g,h PART 3

(You must put in the commas except after VDU and at the end.)

PART 1 VDU 23 tells the computer we wish to store the character shape.

PART 2 The ASCII number is the ASCII code you wish to put your new shape in.

(Sometimes called re-defining a character.) The number we will use is between 224 and 255. This one is number 251.

PART 3 This part has eight values, one for each row of the character.

Let's label each row **a,b,c,d,e,f,g,h**.

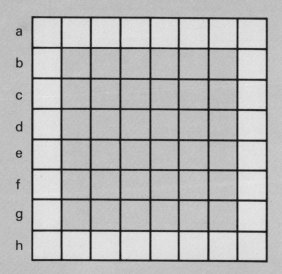

How do we find the value for row **a**, the top row?

The diagram below is of row **a**. Where a square is ON put a **1** and where OFF a **0**. In this row they are all ON:

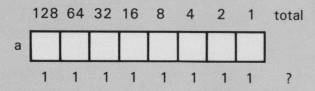

Now this is an 8 bit binary number and we know that 1111 1111 is equal to $128+64+32+16+8+4+2+1$ which equals decimal 255. So the value for row **a** is 255 and we can put this instead of **a** into part 3 of our VDU 23 command.

VDU 23,251,255,b,c,d,e,f,g,h

The other letters can be replaced by values found in the same way:

1 Look at the row in the character block.
2 Put in the ones and noughts.
3 Write this as an 8 bit binary number.
4 Calculate the equivalent decimal value.
5 Put the value in the right place in the VDU 23 command.

Try the next row:

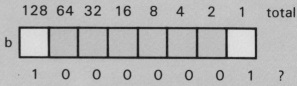

The decimal equivalent of this number is:

$128+0+0+0+0+0+0+1$
so **b** = 129.

24

Our VDU 23 command now looks like this: | VDU 23, **251**, 255,129,c,d,e,f,g,h |

Using **1** for ON and **0** for OFF makes the whole character look like this:

	128	64	32	16	8	4	2	1		total
a	1	1	1	1	1	1	1	1		$128+64+32+16+8+4+2+1 = 255 = a$
b	1	0	0	0	0	0	0	1		$128+ 0 + 0 + 0 +0+0+0+1 = 129 = b$
c	1	0	0	0	0	0	0	1		$128+ 0 + 0 + 0 +0+0+0+1 = 129 = c$
d	1	0	0	0	0	0	0	1		$128+ 0 + 0 + 0 +0+0+0+1 = 129 = d$
e	1	0	0	0	0	0	0	1		$128+ 0 + 0 + 0 +0+0+0+1 = 129 = e$
f	1	0	0	0	0	0	0	1		$128+ 0 + 0 + 0 +0+0+0+1 = 129 = f$
g	1	0	0	0	0	0	0	1		$128+ 0 + 0 + 0 +0+0+0+1 = 129 = g$
h	1	1	1	1	1	1	1	1		$128+64+32+16+8+4+2+1 = 255 = h$

We can print this square in all MODES but MODE 7. Let's use MODE 4. When we want to print the shape or character we can use the method on page 11. We will use the PRINT CHR$(ASCII code) method.

> **THE NUMBERS ABOVE SHOW HOW EACH ROW VALUE IS CALCULATED**

Type in:

```
MODE 4
VDU 23,251,255,129,129,129,129,129,129,255
PRINT CHR$(251)
```

RETURN
RETURN
RETURN

DID IT WORK?

Do you want the square near the middle of the screen?

Then type in:

```
PRINT TAB(20,15)CHR$(251)
``` `RETURN`

Let's try another shape such as an arrow. See the picture below.

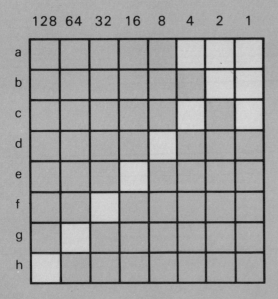

	128	64	32	16	8	4	2	1
a								
b								
c								
d								
e								
f								
g								
h								

If we replace those squares ON with a **1** and those OFF with **0** we get:

	128	64	32	16	8	4	2	1	total
a	0	0	0	0	0	1	1	1	7
b	0	0	0	0	0	0	1	1	3
c	0	0	0	0	0	1	0	1	5
d	0	0	0	0	1	0	0	0	8
e	0	0	0	1	0	0	0	0	16
f	0	0	1	0	0	0	0	0	32
g	0	1	0	0	0	0	0	0	64
h	1	0	0	0	0	0	0	0	128

So we now type in:

```
VDU 23,224,7,3,5,8,16,32,64,128
``` `RETURN`

To print this new character, the arrow, near the centre of the screen type in:

```
MODE4
PRINT TAB(20,15)CHR$(224)
``` `RETURN`

We will now create CHR$(225) with a dot in each corner of the character. We are going to use this shape later. It is easier if you draw it out on paper.

	128	64	32	16	8	4	2	1	total
a	▓							▓	129
b									0
c									0
d									0
e									0
f									0
g									0
h	▓							▓	129

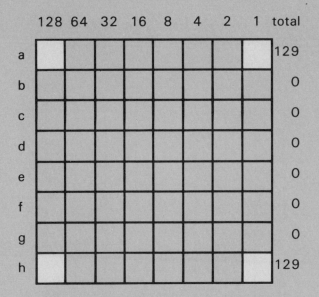

Type in:

```
VDU 23,225,129,0,0,0,0,0,0,129
MODE4
PRINT TAB(20,16)CHR$(225)
```

Let's try to form the letter **H**. Let's look at the computer's **H** more carefully on the screen. Type in our latest character with 4 dots and put 2 **H**s beside it to work out the size of the **H**.

Type in:

```
MODE4
PRINT TAB(20,16)CHR$(225):PRINT
PRINT TAB(21,16)"H";TAB(20,15)"H"
```

You will have to have typed in the VDU 23,225,129,0,0,0,0,0,0,129 line before the rest of the inputs if it is to work. Does your picture look like this?

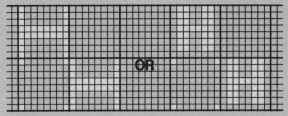

OR

Good! Now we will draw out an H on our 8 by 8 character. Calculate your values for rows **a** to **h** and put them into VDU 23,226,a,b,c,d,e,f,g,h

	128	64	32	16	8	4	2	1	total
a		▓					▓		66
b		▓					▓		?
c		▓					▓		?
d		▓					▓		?
e		▓					▓		?
f		▓					▓		?
g		▓					▓		?
h									0

You work out the code values.

Have you noticed that the H has been drawn so that there is a spare line down each side and across the bottom row?

If the left hand and bottom spaces were not left, all the letters and figures would join together in a single mass without any gaps between the rows of characters, like this:

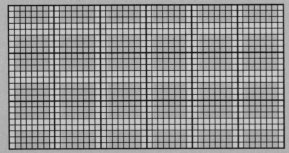

Now we can type in

```
MODE4                          RETURN
VDU 23,226,a,b,c,d,e,f,g,h     RETURN
```

You are now putting your numbers in place of a to h aren't you?

Type in:

```
PRINT TAB(20,16)CHR$(226):PRINT         RETURN
PRINT TAB(21,16)"H";TAB(20,15)"H"        RETURN
```

Has your **H** thin legs
like this?

How can we thicken the legs? We must put in more dots. Let's change it.

	128	64	32	16	8	4	2	1	total
a		1	1			1	1		102
b		1	1			1	1		?
c		1	1			1	1		?
d		1	1	1	1	1	1		?
e		1	1			1	1		?
f		1	1			1	1		?
g		1	1			1	1		?
h									0

NOW YOU CAN WORK OUT THE CODE VALUES

Type in the new VDU 23,227,a,...h code and print it out using CHR$(227).

Your H should now be as good as the computer's.

You could try other simple shapes such as triangles and rectangles.

28

Would you like to make a little figure who can wave or move across the screen?

First you need to draw out the figure you want on the 8 by 8 grid.

Type in:

```
 10 MODE 4
 15 REM Person with arm up
 20 VDU23,228,60,61,25,127,24,126,66,66
 25 REM Person with arm down
 30 VDU23,229,60,60,24,127,25,127,66,66
 40  FOR wave = 1 TO 10
 45 REM Print person with arm up.
 50 PRINT TAB(20,10)CHR$(228)
 60 FOR delay =1 TO 500 :NEXT delay
 65 REM Print person with arm down.
 70 PRINT TAB(20,10)CHR$(229)
 80 FOR delay =1 TO 700 :NEXT delay
 90  NEXT wave
100 END
```

	128	64	32	16	8	4	2	1	total
a			1	1	1	1			60
b			1	1	1	1		1	?
c				1	1			1	?
d		1	1	1	1	1	1	1	?
e				1	1				?
f		1	1	1	1	1	1		?
g		1					1		?
h		1					1		?

You can store this figure with his arm up in code number 228 and his arm down in 229. Let's write a little program to make him wave ten times.

Put in the program and type

RUN RETURN

Can you make him move across the screen?

You need to change the first value in the TAB statement. Don't forget to rub him out as he moves using " " ie typing a space in the right place.

This is a program which will do this.

```
 10 REM Moving waving person.
 20 MODE 4
 30 VDU23,228,60,61,25,127,24,126,66,66
 40 VDU23,229,60,60,24,127,25,127,66,66
 50  FOR X=1 TO 30 STEP 2
 55 REM Print person with arm up.
 60 PRINT TAB(X,10)CHR$(228)
 70 FOR delay =1 TO 300 :NEXT delay
 75 REM Print blank over person.
 80 PRINT TAB(X,10)" "
 85 REM Print person with arm down.
 90 PRINT TAB(X+1,10)CHR$(229)
100 FOR delay =1 TO 300 :NEXT delay
105 REM Print blank over person.
110 PRINT TAB(X+1,10)" "
120  NEXT X
130 END
```

AND, OR and EOR

We are familiar with BITS and BYTES and we are now going to look at another topic which requires an understanding of bits known by computer people as *bit by bit* or *bitwise* operations.

This topic will be very useful to you when you start designing programs using colour graphics with the GCOL statement or when you use your microcomputer to control things.

AND

Let's consider two bulbs A and B. A is a red bulb and B is a green bulb. As on page 2 if a bulb is ON we will say it is in logic state 1 and if OFF, logic state 0.

The drawing below shows all the possible combinations of ONs and OFFs for the two bulbs.

We can now look at each combination and see in which column the red lamp *and* the green lamp are ON.

A	1	0	1	0
B	1	1	0	0
A AND B	1	0	0	0

If they are both on we put a 1 in the AND row, if not then we put a 0 as shown above.

Now consider two numbers in binary, such as 2 and 3.

	decimal	binary
2	2	10
3	3	11
2 AND 3	2	10

If we AND the right bit of each number we get 0 AND 1 which gives 0. If we AND the left bits we get 1 AND 1 which gives 1 as shown above.

Now binary 10 is decimal 2 so if we AND 2 and 3 we get 2. Let's try it on the computer.

Type in

PRINT 2 AND 3   RETURN

DID YOU GET 2?
YOU NOW KNOW WHY!

OR

Let's now look at the OR function. Consider the red and green bulbs on the opposite page. This time we will consider under which conditions the red OR the green bulb is ON.

Note that OR in this case is not quite the same as 'or' as used in normal English. If the red bulb is ON or the green bulb is ON we put a 1 in the OR column.

A	1	0	1	0
B	1	1	0	0
A OR B	1	1	1	0

So logical OR is true if *either* or *both* lights are ON.

An example of the OR condition occurs in most cars. The interior light of a car comes on if just the front offside door or just the front nearside door are open or both front doors are open.

Let us now OR two numbers bit by bit. We can use 2 and 3.

If we OR the right bit of each number we get 0 OR 1 = 1. The left bits give 1 OR 1 = 1.

	decimal	binary
2	2	10
3	3	11
2 OR 3	?	11

So if we OR 2 and 3 we get 3.

You can now try 3 bit numbers. What is 5 OR 3?

We get

	decimal	binary
5	5	101
3	3	011
5 OR 3	?	111

Type in: PRINT 5 OR 3 RETURN

Do you get 5 OR 3 equals 7?

EOR

EOR stands for Exclusive OR, sometimes abbreviated XOR. The Exclusive OR (EOR) behaves in the same way as 'or' in the English language.

Consider the bulbs on page 30 again.

We put a 1 in the EOR column only when either the red bulb or the green bulb is ON.

A	1	0	1	0
B	1	1	0	0
A EOR B	0	1	1	0

Let us now EOR two numbers bit by bit. We can use the same two numbers as before, 2 and 3.

If we EOR the right bit of each number we get 0 EOR 1 = 1. The next left bits give 1 EOR 1 = 0.

So 2 EOR 3 equals 1.

	decimal	binary
2	2	10
3	3	11
2 EOR 3	?	01

Try this on your computer.

DO YOU NOW UNDERSTAND THE MEANING OF THE LOGIC TERMS AND, OR AND EXCLUSIVE OR ?

If you don't, practise some more and check them using your computer.

You will find these terms used in digital electronics, as well as colour graphics.